BALLPARK GREATS

PRO BASEBALL'S BEST PLAYERS

MAX
SCHERZER

DONALD PARKER

BALLPARK GREATS

PRO BASEBALL'S BEST PLAYERS

CHRISTIAN YELICH

JUSTIN VERLANDER

MAX SCHERZER

MIKE TROUT

NOLAN ARENADO

BALLPARK GREATS

PRO BASEBALL'S BEST PLAYERS

MAX SCHERZER

DONALD PARKER

MASON CREST
PHILADELPHIA
MIAMI

Mason Crest
450 Parkway Drive, Suite D
Broomall, Pennsylvania 19008
(866) MCP-BOOK (toll-free)
www.masoncrest.com

First printing
9 8 7 6 5 4 3 2 1

ISBN (hardback) 978-1-4222-4439-5
ISBN (series) 978-1-4222-4434-0
ISBN (ebook) 978-1-4222-7374-6

Library of Congress Cataloging-in-Publication Data

Names: Parker, Donald, author. | Mason Crest Publishers.
Title: Max Scherzer / Donald Parker
Description: Broomall, Pennsylvania : Mason Crest, 2020. | Series: Ballpark
  Greats: Pro baseball's best players | Includes webography. | Includes
  bibliographical references and index.
Identifiers: LCCN 2019034456 | ISBN 9781422244395 (Hardback) | ISBN
  9781422273746 (eBook) | ISBN 9781422244340 (Series)
Subjects: LCSH: Scherzer, Max, 1984—Juvenile literature. | Baseball
  players—United States—Biography—Juvenile literature.
Classification: LCC GV865.S3525 P37 2020 | DDC 796.357092 [B]—dc23
LC record available at https://lccn.loc.gov/2019034456

Developed and Produced by National Highlights Inc.
Editor: Andrew Luke
Production: Crafted Content LLC

NATIONAL
HIGHLIGHTS

QR CODES AND LINKS TO THIRD-PARTY CONTENT

CONTENTS

KEY ICONS TO LOOK FOR:

Words to Understand: These words with their easy-to-understand definitions will increase the reader's understanding of the text, while building vocabulary skills.

Sidebars: This boxed material within the main text allows readers to build knowledge, gain insights, explore possibilities, and broaden their perspectives by weaving together additional information to provide realistic and holistic perspectives.

Educational Videos: Readers can view videos by scanning our QR codes, providing them with additional educational content to supplement the text. Examples include news coverage, moments in history, speeches, iconic sports moments, and much more!

Text-Dependent Questions: These questions send the reader back to the text for more careful attention to the evidence presented there.

Research Projects: Readers are pointed toward areas of further inquiry connected to each chapter. Suggestions are provided for projects that encourage deeper research and analysis.

Series Glossary of Key Terms: This back-of-the-book glossary contains terminology used throughout this series. Words found here increase the reader's ability to read and comprehend higher-level books and articles in this field.

WORDS TO UNDERSTAND

debut: a first appearance

enshrine: to preserve or cherish as sacred

exclusive: available to only a few people because of high barriers to entr

immaculate: having or containing no flaw or error

stint: a period of time spent at a particular activity

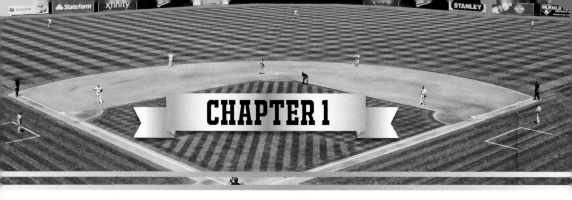

CHAPTER 1

GREATEST MOMENTS

MAX SCHERZER'S
MAJOR LEAGUE BASEBALL CAREER

Max Scherzer, or Mad Max as he is known around the league, is one of the best pitchers in all of Major League Baseball (MLB). He began his career, after three years pitching for the Tigers of the University of Missouri at Columbia, as a pitcher for the Arizona Diamondbacks in 2008. After a two-year **stint** in Arizona, Scherzer was traded to Detroit, Michigan, where he teamed up with right-handed pitching ace Justin Verlander (now of the Houston Astros). He spent five seasons in Detroit, appearing in the 2012 World Series against San Francisco.

Scherzer's first appearance came in a relief effort on April 29, 2008, against the Houston Astros. He pitched four and a third innings and struck out seven batters. The effort left Scherzer one strikeout short of the league's record for strikeouts by a reliever making his **debut**. He won the first of two Cy Young Awards as a member of the Tigers in 2013. During his time in Detroit, Scherzer helped lead the Tigers to four straight American League (AL) Central Division titles (2011–2014) and the American League pennant in 2012.

Scherzer, through the 2019 season, has won 162 games in 351 appearances and 342 starts. He is a member of the 2,500-strikeout club and is within striking distance of reaching 3,000 for his career. He is ranked just behind Yankees hurler C. C. Sabathia (3,028) and former teammate Verlander (2,809) in active career strikeouts. He has a career 3.22 earned run average (ERA) and a walks and hits per inning pitched (WHIP) over a nine-inning average of 1.128, including four consecutive seasons of a WHIP that was below one. This means that Scherzer allows few batters to reach base. He is regarded as one of the nastiest pitchers in the league and most feared to face.

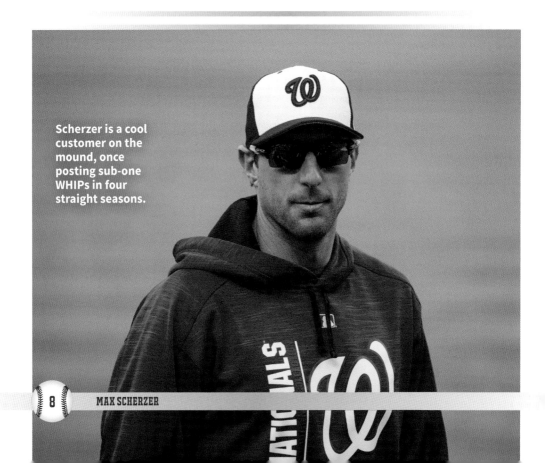

Scherzer is a cool customer on the mound, once posting sub-one WHIPs in four straight seasons.

GREATEST CAREER MOMENTS

HERE IS A LIST OF SOME OF SCHERZER'S CAREER FIRSTS AND GREATEST ACHIEVEMENTS DURING HIS TIME IN MLB:

PITCHED FIRST CAREER NO-HITTER

Scherzer, as a member of the Washington Nationals, threw MLB's 289th no-hitter. Playing against the Pittsburgh Pirates on June 20, 2015, he set down the first 26 batters he faced before hitting pinch hitter Jose Tabata with a pitch, sending him to first base. Tabata was the second of only two batters to see a base (the other runner reached as a result of a walk) as he set down the next batter he faced (Josh Harrison) to complete the no-hitter. For the game, Scherzer struck out 10 batters, gave up a walk, and recorded the complete game victory as the Nationals beat the Pirates 6–0.

Scherzer recovers from hitting a Pittsburgh batter in the top of the ninth on his way to completing his first career no-hitter.

PITCHED FIRST CAREER IMMACULATE INNING

An **immaculate** inning occurs when a pitcher throws nine pitches in an inning, resulting in three strikeouts and three outs. In a May 14, 2017, game against the Philadelphia Phillies, three days after Red Sox ace Craig Kimbrel struck out three Brewers hitters with nine straight pitches on May 11, Scherzer faced and mowed down Phillies batters Cesar Hernandez, Odubel Herrera, and Aaron Altherr to record his first career immaculate inning. He repeated this in a June 5, 2018, game against the Tampa Bay Rays. This made Scherzer the fifth pitcher in major league history, joining Hall of Fame pitchers Robert "Lefty" Grove, Sandy Koufax, Nolan Ryan, and Randy Johnson, as the only pitchers to have pitched more than one immaculate inning in their career.

Scherzer faced three Philadelphia batters and threw nine pitches for three strikeouts, completing his first career immaculate inning.

TIED THE MAJOR LEAGUE RECORD FOR MOST STRIKEOUTS IN A GAME

Scherzer tied one of the most difficult records to reach for a pitcher in major league baseball. He faced his old Detroit Tigers team in a May 11, 2016, game as a member of the Washington Nationals. Pitching a complete nine-inning game, he struck out 20 Tigers batters on the way to a 3–2 victory. Notably, the 20 strikeouts tied him for the major league record for the most strikeouts by a pitcher in a nine-inning game. His effort tied two other pitchers, Roger Clemens, who accomplished the task twice in 1986 and 1996, and former Chicago Cubs ace Kerry Woods, who struck out 20 Houston Astros players in a May 6, 1998, game.

Watch every strikeout that Scherzer recorded in a May 11, 2016, game against the Detroit Tigers, which tied him for the major league record for strikeouts in a nine-inning game.

TIED MAJOR LEAGUE RECORD FOR CONSECUTIVE SEASONS WITH 250 OR MORE STRIKEOUTS

The ability to strike out another team's batters is one of the measurements used to determine the success of a pitcher. Scherzer, through the 2019 season, has struck out 2,692 batters. This places him third among active pitchers and 24th on the career strikeout list. From his last season with the Detroit Tigers through the 2018 season, he struck out at least 250 players in each season. With an average of 276 strikeouts, he threw nearly half of his career total over that five-year span. He became only the fourth pitcher in major league history (along with Ferguson Jenkins, Pedro Martinez, and Randy Johnson) to have pitched five consecutive seasons with 250 or more strikeouts in each.

Take a look at the five seasons, 2014–2018, in which Scherzer recorded at least 250 strikeouts in a season, to join an exclusive club of pitchers.

WON AMERICAN LEAGUE CY YOUNG AWARD

Scherzer recorded his first career 20+ win season in 2013 as a member of the Detroit Tigers. His 21-win, three-loss effort, along with a 2.90 earned run average (ERA), 240 strikeouts, and WHIP of 0.972 earned him not only his first All-Star appearance but also the vote of the Baseball Writers' Association of America (BWAA) as the AL Cy Young Award winner. His effort in 2013, coming off his appearance in the 2012 World Series, helped return the Tigers to the AL Championship Series, which they lost to the Boston Red Sox. This award was the last Cy Young he would win in the AL but not the last Cy Young Award he would win.

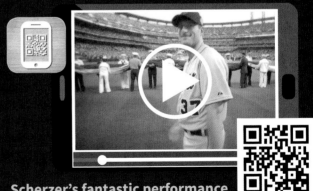

Scherzer's fantastic performance in 2013 led to his winning his first career Cy Young Award as a member of the Detroit Tigers.

WON NATIONAL LEAGUE CY YOUNG AWARD

Scherzer joined the Washington Nationals in a return to the National League (NL) in 2015. After a solid debut for the team, which resulted in a 2015 season that saw him win 14 games and lose 12 with an ERA of 2.80 and 276 strikeouts, he came back in 2016 even better. A 20–7 win–loss record (for his second career 20-win season) and 284 strikeouts, as well as a sub-1.000 WHIP (0.969) gave him what he needed to lock down the second Cy Young Award of his career and first in the NL. Scherzer would go on to win a consecutive BWAA NL Cy Young Award in the 2017 season.

A video compiled by the *Washington Post* shows the numbers that helped Scherzer win the 2016 NL Cy Young Award, the first of two NL Cy Youngs he has won in his career.

WON FIRST WORLD SERIES CHAMPIONSHIP

It is no coincidence that in Scherzer's first 12 seasons, his teams went to the post season seven times. For Scherzer, the seventh time was the charm. Scherzer went 3-0 in the 2019 post season, including 1-0 in the World Series against Houston. He posted a 3.60 ERA with 10 strikeouts over 10 total innings, including a Game 1 win. It was a seven game series in which the road team won every game, an MLB first. Scherzer was most effective in the NLDS against the LA Dodgers and the NLCS against St. Louis, where he gave up a total of one run in a combined 15 innings to lead the Nationals to the World Series. He picked up 21 strikeouts in those 15 innings. Washington made the post season as a wild card team, and faced the Milwaukee Brewers in a one-game playoff to advance to the NLDS. Manager Dave Martinez elected to go with Scherzer as his starter for this critical game, which the Nationals won 4-3. This was the first World Series championship for a Washington D.C.-based team since the 1924 Washington Senators.

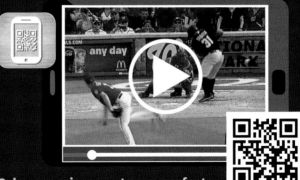

Scherzer misses out on a perfect game in a June 20, 2015, effort against the Pittsburgh Pirates but takes comfort in winning his 100th career game.

REACHED 2,500 CAREER STRIKEOUTS (APRIL 26, 2019)

In an April 26, 2019, home game against the San Diego Padres, Scherzer pitched seven innings in a losing effort. He gave up four hits and two earned runs, including a home run, resulting in an ERA of 2.57. He struck out 10 batters in the game. The sixth strikeout brought him to the number 2,500 for his career. This placed him third among active career pitchers in the major leagues (as of June 2, 2019) behind Verlander (second) and Sabathia (first), and 29th on the all-time list. He is the third-fastest pitcher in league history to reach 2,500 strikeouts in a career.

Scherzer, pitching in the sixth inning against the Padres, throws three pitches that result in a strikeout of San Diego outfielder Manuel Margot, his 2,500th career strikeout.

Scherzer is one of only six pitchers in the history of baseball who has won the Cy Young Award in both the AL and NL. He joins pitching greats Roger Clemens, Roy Halladay, Randy Johnson, Pedro Martinez, and Gaylord Perry. Johnson, Martinez, and Perry are all members of the Hall of Fame, whereas Clemens, Johnson, Martinez, and Perry all have finished their careers with 3,000 or more strikeouts (Clemens, with 4,672 strikeouts, is ranked third all time, whereas Johnson at 4,875 strikeouts is second only to Hall of Famer Nolan Ryan).

Scherzer is one of only seven pitchers to have pitched multiple career immaculate innings.

The way Scherzer has pitched the ball in his first 12 major league seasons has put him in **exclusive** company. There is no reason to suspect that as long as he is healthy and making quality starts, he will not someday see himself **enshrined** in Cooperstown, New York, and given a place of honor with the best to have ever thrown the baseball. On his way to the Hall of Fame, he will have struck out more than 3,000 hitters and won close to, if not more than, 300 games, both lofty goals for a pitcher of any talent level.

TEXT-DEPENDENT QUESTIONS

1. How many no-hitters has Scherzer pitched in his major league career? What was the date he pitched his first no-hitter? What team was that no-hitter against?

2. Through the 2019 season, how many strikeouts had Scherzer recorded in his career? How many consecutive seasons has he thrown 250 or more strikeouts?

3. What season did he win his first Cy Young Award? How many Cy Young Awards has Scherzer won in his career?

RESEARCH PROJECT

Scherzer's pitching career has placed him in the company of some of the best pitchers ever seen in MLB. He has recorded 250 or more strikeouts over six consecutive seasons (2014–2019), joining three other pitchers in history. He has led his respective leagues in wins four times. He also won the Cy Young three times and joined the 2,500-strikeout club in the 2019 season. Looking at the multiple Cy Young winners in MLB history, compare their career stats to see which pitchers have the most strikeouts and career wins and which made the most All-Star appearances, ranking each in order in those three categories.

WORDS TO UNDERSTAND

distinction: an accomplishment that sets one apart

fierce: furiously active or determined

prestigious: having standing or estimation in the eyes of people; weight or credit in general opinion

relegate: to put (someone or something) in a lower or less important position, rank, etc.

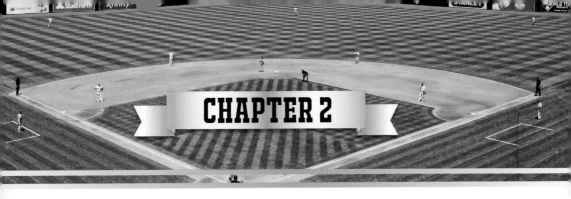

CHAPTER 2

THE ROAD TO THE TOP

SCHERZER'S PLAYER PERFORMANCE

Maxwell M. Scherzer (there is no information about what his middle name is, just the initial "M") was born on July 27, 1984, in Chesterfield, Missouri. Chesterfield is a suburb of St. Louis. He is the oldest of two children, with a younger brother Alex, who was born five years later. Scherzer was a fan of the St. Louis Cardinals and grew up watching Cardinals baseball, with the dream of taking the field at Busch Stadium one day to join the greats who have played in that historic ballpark.

Scherzer attended high school at Parkway Central High School in Chesterfield. Although he wasn't the best athlete on the team, he was **fiercely** competitive, which helped him early on become the player he was when he entered the major leagues. Scherzer was drafted by the St. Louis Cardinals in the 2003 draft out of high school but declined to play for the team and instead chose to attend the University of Missouri. His decision to delay entry into the major leagues and attend college instead proved to be an important one in his development. It helped Scherzer further develop the skills that he displays with every major league start.

Scherzer chose to attend the University of Missouri after he was not drafted until the 43rd round by St. Louis in 2003.

Scherzer entered the University of Missouri ("Mizzou") in the fall of 2003, intent on showing everybody that he was ready to play baseball at the next level. His career at Mizzou (nicknamed the Tigers) produced some impressive results, gaining Scherzer many awards and national recognition. After 13 appearances in his freshman year, including two starts, Scherzer came back to lead the Tigers and the Big 12 Conference with a 1.87 ERA in his sophomore season. He also led the conference with 131 strikeouts, which broke a 14-year school record for strikeouts in a season. He made such an impression in his sophomore year that he was named a second team All-American and to the All Big 12 Conference team. Scherzer was also named the Big 12 Pitcher of the Year, winning nine games against four losses with a WHIP of 0.94.

Although injuries caused Scherzer to slow down a bit in his junior year, his pitching performance for the Tigers was enough to make Scherzer the highest drafted University of Missouri player to ever be selected in baseball's amateur draft. He was drafted with the 11th pick of the 2006 draft by the Arizona Diamondbacks. He joined an Arizona team that would a year later add to its rosters one of the greatest pitchers in major league history, Randy Johnson. Scherzer, who eventually was traded to Detroit and the Washington Nationals, shares with Johnson the **distinction** of being one of only 10 major league pitchers to win the **prestigious** Cy Young Award three or more times.

Hall-of-Fame left hander Randy Johnson is one of only nine pitchers other than Scherzer to ever win at least three Cy Young awards.

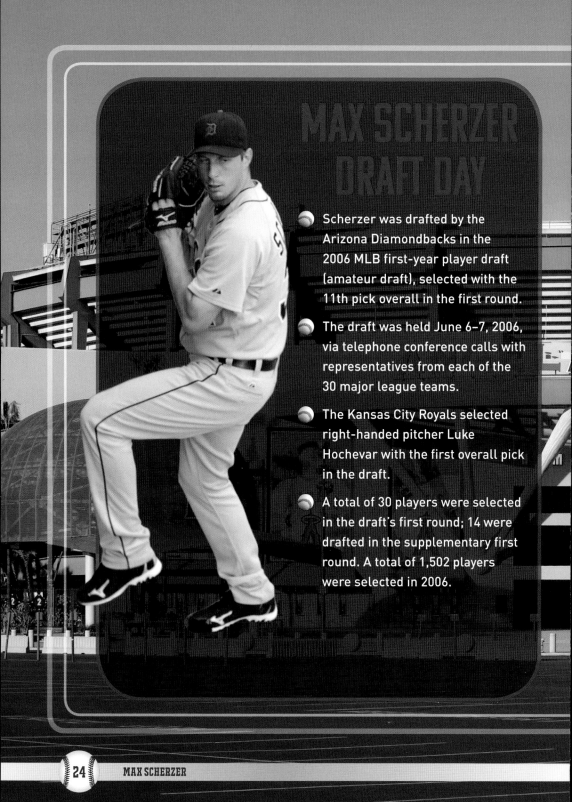

MAX SCHERZER
DRAFT DAY

- Scherzer was drafted by the Arizona Diamondbacks in the 2006 MLB first-year player draft (amateur draft), selected with the 11th pick overall in the first round.

- The draft was held June 6–7, 2006, via telephone conference calls with representatives from each of the 30 major league teams.

- The Kansas City Royals selected right-handed pitcher Luke Hochevar with the first overall pick in the draft.

- A total of 30 players were selected in the draft's first round; 14 were drafted in the supplementary first round. A total of 1,502 players were selected in 2006.

2006 DRAFT DAY SIGNIFICANT ACCOUNTS

- Four players who were selected in the 2006 amateur draft chose to play in the National Football League: Riley Cooper (157th pick, Philadelphia Phillies), Jake Locker (1,212th pick, Los Angeles Angels), Isaiah Stanback (1,342nd pick, Baltimore Orioles), and Kyle Williams (1,417th pick, Chicago White Sox). Stanback, a wide receiver (WR) for the New York Giants, was a member of the team that won Super Bowl XLVI in 2011; Williams, also a WR for the Denver Broncos, was a member of the Broncos squad that won Super Bowl L in 2014.

- Scherzer was the eighth of 18 pitchers selected in the first round. None has pitched more major league games than Scherzer.

- Two other Cy Young winners (along with multiple winner Max Scherzer) were drafted in 2006: Tim Lincecum (San Francisco Giants) won the NL award in 2008 and 2009, and Clayton Kershaw (Los Angeles Dodgers) won the NL Cy Young Award in 2011, 2013, and 2014, and also the 2014 NL Most Valuable Player (MVP).

- The first player from the 2006 draft to play in the major leagues was pitcher Andrew Miller of the Detroit Tigers, who appeared in relief in a game on August 30, 2006.

- The Boston Red Sox had four first-round selections in 2006 (outfielder [OF] Jason Pace, 27th pick; right-handed pitcher [RHP] Daniel Bard, 28th pick; left-handed pitcher [LHP] Kris Johnson, 40th pick; and RHP Caleb Clay, 44th pick).

ATHLETIC ACCOMPLISHMENTS

HIGH SCHOOL

Scherzer attended Parkway Central High School (nickname: Colts) from 1999 to 2003 in his hometown of Chesterfield. He played baseball and basketball for Parkway Central. Scherzer played all four years at Parkway as a member of the varsity squad. He pitched in 38 games for the Colts, making 28 starts. He posted an overall 15–14 record.

Scherzer began coming into his own in his junior and sophomore years, with 72 strikeouts in each of those seasons for Parkway Central. He began learning how to throw to overpower hitters, resulting in a dip in his ERA from the 5.00 to 6.00 range to the mid-2s by the time he left Parkway in 2003.

Scherzer's pitching stats for his time at Parkway Central are summarized in the following table:

Year	Class	W	L	W-L%	ERA	GP	GS	IP	H	R	ER	HR	SO
2000	Freshman	2	4	0.333	6.68	8	4	22.0	35	37	21	2	22
2001	Sophomore	2	5	0.286	4.89	10	7	39.3	54	34	28	1	13
2002	Junior	6	3	0.667	2.80	9	9	50.0	43	26	20	0	72
2003	Senior	5	2	0.714	2.32	11	8	45.3	27	18	15	2	72
TOTALS		15	14	0.517	4.83	38	28	156.6	159	115	84	5	179

COLLEGE

Scherzer passed on being drafted by the Cardinals in 2003 to attend the University of Missouri. He was initially **relegated** to the relief staff as a freshman. Scherzer appeared in 13 games, getting the opportunity to start two and posting a 0–1 record. It was in his sophomore year that he found his rhythm and confidence, helping the Tigers win 40 games for the first time in 14 seasons (since 1991). He was part of a multiple pitcher effort in a game against Texas Tech on April 1, 2005, that resulted in a no-hitter. Scherzer's sophomore season also resulted in his being named a semi-finalist for the Roger Clemens Award, an award given to the best pitcher in college. The award is named for former University of Texas Longhorn and MLB superstar pitcher Roger Clemens.

Scherzer played his home games in college at Taylor Stadium in Columbia, Missouri.

MISSOURI TIGERS

Scherzer capped his collegiate career with a strong pitching performance over the then number one Florida Gators of the Southeastern Conference (SEC) in his junior year. He also pitched a seven-inning shutout of powerhouse University of Oklahoma (nickname: Sooners) in the Big 12 Conference tournament. Scherzer's arm helped lead the Tigers to their first National Collegiate Athletic Association College World Series Regional tournament win before falling to Cal-State Fullerton in the Super Regionals.

Scherzer's stats for his three years at the University of Missouri are summarized in the table that follows:

Year	Class	W	L	W-L%	ERA	GP	GS	IP	H	R	ER	HR	BB	SO	WHIP
2004	Freshman	0	1	0.000	5.85	13	2	20	19	17	13	1	16	23	1.75
2005	Sophomore	9	4	0.692	1.87	16	16	106	59	26	22	3	41	131	0.94
2006	Junior	7	3	0.700	2.25	14	13	80	57	22	20	3	23	78	1.00
TOTALS		16	8	0.667	2.40	43	31	206	135	65	55	7	80	232	1.04

Scherzer decided to pass on his senior year with the Tigers and try his luck in the 2006 amateur draft. Waiting three years paid off for Scherzer when he received a vote of confidence from the Arizona Diamondbacks, who used their first pick in the first round of the draft (number 11 overall) to select him.

BECOMING "MAD MAX"

Scherzer came out of high school prepared to learn what it takes to become a great major league pitcher. He chose to attend the University of Missouri (nickname: Tigers) in 2003 and began to take the mound, first as a reliever in his freshman year and then as a part of the starting staff in his sophomore year. It was as a sophomore that he began to show signs of becoming Mad Max, a nickname that was first given to him in college because of his fierce competitive nature. The nickname has stuck with him ever since. He struck out 131 batters in 2005, displaying masterful control, speed, and power. His strikeout total is the most of any Mizzou pitcher in school history and put him on the path to future success from the mound later in his career.

Scherzer's reputation as one of the nastiest hurlers in MLB all began from his days as a member of the University of Missouri Tigers pitching staff from 2004 to 2006.

MINOR LEAGUE BASEBALL

After accepting a $3 million signing bonus from the Diamondbacks, Scherzer was assigned to play for the team's minor league affiliate in Mobile, Alabama. Interestingly, Diamondbacks Scouting Director Mike Rizzo, who was instrumental in drafting Scherzer with the team's first pick, would be part of the team that convinced him to leave Detroit and come to Washington eight years later in 2014, when Rizzo was general manager of the Nationals.

Nationals general manager Mike Rizzo is a big believer in Scherzer. Not only did Rizzo trade for Scherzer to bring him to the Nationals, but he also recommended drafting Scherzer when he was scouting director in Arizona.

Scherzer made 14 appearances in 2007 for double-A Mobile (nickname: BayBears) in the Southern League. He won four games against four losses with 76 strikeouts. His effort was enough to move him to stops in Visalia, California (Visalia Oaks), of the A+ California League; Scottsdale, Arizona (Scottsdale Scorpions) in the Arizona League; and double-A Fort Worth, Texas (Fort Worth Cats). Scherzer's low WHIP and ERA for each of these stops, coupled with 73 total strikeouts over 45.2 innings pitched, shortened his minor league career and earned him an early appearance in the major leagues beginning in 2008 in a relief appearance against the Houston Astros.

Between 2008 and 2010, Scherzer made a total of 20 more minor league appearances while also pitching for the Diamondbacks and Detroit Tigers

Teddy, the mascot for the Mobile BayBears, cheered for Scherzer when he played for the team in 2007.

(he was traded to Detroit in 2010). His results in his minor league stint are summarized in the following table:

Year	Tm-Class	W	L	W-L%	ERA	G	GS	SV	IP	H	R	ER	HR	BB	SO	WHIP
2007	Mobile-AA	4	4	0.500	3.93	14	14	0	73.2	64	38	32	3	40	76	1.421
2007	Visalia-A+	2	0	1.000	0.53	3	3	0	17.0	5	1	1	0	2	30	0.412
2007	Scottsdale-Fall	1	1	0.500	2.21	8	0	0	12.2	6	5	3	1	5	18	0.902
2007	Fort Worth-Independent	1	0	1.000	0.56	3	3	0	16.0	9	2	1	0	4	25	0.813
2008	Tucson-AAA	1	1	0.500	2.72	13	10	0	53.0	35	19	16	2	22	79	1.075
2008	Phoenix-Fall	1	0	1.000	3.38	4	4	0	24.0	16	10	9	3	5	24	0.875
2009	Visalia-A+	0	0	0.000	2.14	1	1	0	4.2	1	2	1	0	4	5	1.190
2010	Toledo-AAA	2	0	1.000	0.60	2	2	0	15.0	4	1	1	0	2	17	0.400
TOTALS		12	6	0.667	2.68	48	37	0	214.6	140	78	64	9	84	274	1.044

TEXT-DEPENDENT QUESTIONS

1. What team drafted Scherzer in 2003?

2. How many strikeouts did Scherzer record in his college career?

3. How many total wins did Scherzer have during his three years at the University of Missouri? How many total wins did he record during his time in the minor leagues?

RESEARCH PROJECT

The St. Louis Cardinals, his hometown team, initially drafted Scherzer in the 2003 amateur baseball draft. He chose instead to attend the University of Missouri, where he became an All-American and All-Conference pitcher and was eventually selected in the first round of the 2006 draft by the Arizona Diamondbacks. Looking at the pitchers in the league who were drafted in the first round over the past 25 seasons, make a list of those who were drafted by their hometown team.

WORDS TO UNDERSTAND

imposing: impressive in size, bearing, dignity, or grandeur

mystique: a special quality that makes a person or thing interesting or exciting

toil: long strenuous fatiguing labor

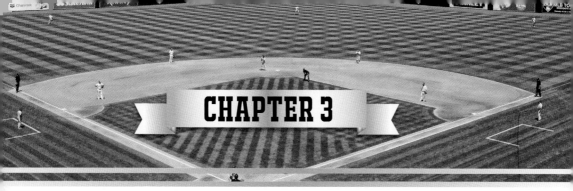

CHAPTER 3

ON THE DIAMOND

ON THE FIELD ACCOMPLISHMENTS

Scherzer is six feet three inches (1.91 m) tall. That certainly gives him an **imposing** presence on the mound, but the most intimidating thing about Scherzer is not his fastball or will to win, but rather his two different-colored eyes. He was born with a condition called heterochromia iridis, which causes Scherzer to have one blue and one brown eye. Having different-colored eyes certainly plays into his Mad Max **mystique** and may have contributed to him becoming a dominant pitcher. Scherzer is one of a handful of famous people who was born with heterochromia iridis. The condition, which is not harmful in any way, results in a unique look for the three-time Cy Young winner, and his one blue and one brown eye work perfectly well for him to see the pitches he throws to rack up strikeouts.

Scherzer made his first MLB start for the Arizona Diamondbacks in a game on April 29, 2008, against the Houston Astros. He tied a record for strikeouts (seven) by a Diamondbacks pitcher in his debut game on April 29, 2008, against the Houston Astros. He has subsequently been recognized as follows:

- Named MLB Pitcher of the Month, NL, five times
- Named MLB Player of the Week, NL, three times; AL, once
- Won Cy Young Award three times, AL (2013) and NL (2016–2017)
- Named *The Sporting News* Pitcher of the Year three times, AL (2013) and NL (2016–2017)

Scherzer had a career ERA of 3.22 through the 2019 season. Winning the National League Cy Young Award in 2016 made him the sixth pitcher to win the award in both leagues. He went on to win the award again in 2017 as a member of the Washington Nationals, making him one of only seven pitchers in MLB's history to win the award in consecutive seasons. His 1.100 WHIP is one of the lowest among active pitchers.

Scherzer won the 2013 AL Cy Young award when he went 21-3 with the Detroit Tigers.

MAX SCHERZER

MAX SCHERZER
Washington Nationals
CAREER STATS

GP	GS	Wins	Losses	ERA	SO	BB
365	356	170	89	3.20	2,692	618

PITCHER

- Date of birth: July 27, 1984

- Height: Six feet three inches (1.91 m), Weight: 215 pounds (97 kg)

- 2019 World Series Champion

- Three-time Cy Young Award winner (2013, 2016, and 2017)

- Seven-time MLB All-Star (2013–2019)

- MLB record holder for strikeouts in a nine-inning game (20)

- 250-plus strikeouts in an MLB record five consecutive seasons (2014–2018)

- Four-time league leader in wins (2013, 2014, 2016, and 2018)

- Four-time NL leader in strikeouts (2016–2019)

- Four-time league leader in WHIP (2013 and 2016–2018)

Other recognitions and accomplishments in Scherzer's career include the following:

- Major league leader in wins four times: AL twice (2013, 2014) and NL twice (2016, 2018)
- The third-fastest pitcher in major league history to reach 2,500 strikeouts
- Leader in AL in win–loss% in 2013 (87.5%)
- Major league leader in WHIP four times: AL once (2013) and NL three times (2016–2018)
- NL leader in strikeouts three times (2016–2018)

Scherzer's first MLB appearance came at Arizona's Chase Field in relief against the Houston Astros.

CAREER TOTALS

Scherzer made his first appearance in the major leagues as a member of the Arizona Diamondbacks in 2008. He has since appeared in 351 games, starting in 342 of them. He has a career 162 wins and 87 losses for a career win–loss percentage of 65.1%. He is also ranked third on the active player career strikeout list with 2,566 Ks as of June 2, 2019. His totals, through 2,199.5

innings pitched, put him on track to reach 3,000 strikeouts over his next 246 innings or at about the beginning of the 2021 season.

Here is a look at Scherzer's year-to-year totals since his first appearance in 2008:

Year	W	L	W-L%	ERA	G	GS	IP	H	R	ER	HR	BB	SO	WHIP
2008	0	4	0.000	3.05	16	7	56.0	48	24	19	5	21	66	1.232
2009	9	11	0.450	4.13	30	30	170.1	166	94	78	20	63	174	1.346
2010	12	11	0.522	3.50	31	31	195.2	174	84	76	20	70	184	1.250
2011	15	9	0.625	4.43	33	33	195.0	207	101	96	29	56	174	1.349
2012	16	7	0.696	3.75	32	32	187.2	179	82	78	23	60	231	1.277
2013	**21**	3	**0.875**	2.90	32	32	214.1	152	73	69	18	56	240	**0.972**
2014	**18**	5	0.783	3.15	33	33	220.1	196	80	77	18	63	252	1.177
2015	14	12	0.538	2.80	33	33	228.2	176	74	71	27	34	276	0.920
2016	**20**	7	0.741	2.96	34	34	**228.1**	165	77	75	31	56	**284**	**0.969**
2017	16	6	0.727	2.52	31	31	200.2	126	62	56	22	55	**268**	**0.904**
2018	**18**	7	0.720	2.53	33	33	**220.2**	150	66	62	23	51	**300**	0.913
2019	11	7	0.611	2.92	27	27	172.1	144	59	56	18	33	**243**	1.027
TOTALS	170	89	0.656	3.20	365	356	2290.0	1883	876	813	254	618	2692	1.092

Bold indicates season(s) in which Scherzer led either the AL or NL in that statistical category

Scherzer is an emotional pitcher, which is in part why he earned the nickname Mad Max in college. He is a fierce competitor who wants to perform well every time he takes the mound. He also likes to work out of jams and bad situations and put his team in a better position to win. In a June 2, 2019, game against the Cincinnati Reds, Washington led 4–1 in the eighth inning with two out. Reds slugger Joey Votto was due to hit, having already doubled off Scherzer earlier in the game. Nationals manager Davey Martinez attempted to remove him from the game, which was met with a defiant no as he approached the mound. Scherzer was responsible for a runner on second and emphatically convinced Martinez he could get Votto. The result? He struck Votto out on three pitches. The Nationals won the game by the score of 4–1, and Scherzer picked up the win, striking out 15.

Mad Max is willing to stand up to his manager and refuse to give up the ball as he stays in a June 2, 2019, game to record a win against the Cincinnati Reds.

PLAYOFF TOTALS

Scherzer has played in 22 career playoff games with Detroit and Washington. He has appeared in the AL Divisional Series four times and the NL Divisional Series three times (as a member of the Washington Nationals). He also made appearance in the AL Championship Series in three consecutive seasons (2011–2013) and advanced to the World Series twice in his career.

Scherzer made his first World Series appearance in 2012. He was a member of the Tigers AL champion team (along with pitching ace and teammate Justin Verlander) that faced off against the NL champions San Francisco Giants. He pitched six and one-third innings for the Tigers, giving up seven hits and three runs and walking a batter. He did strike out eight Giants batters but gave up a home run. His performance resulted in an ERA of 4.43 and a 4–3 loss in game four of the series. Scherzer did not receive a decision for the game. In 2019 he made two World Series starts, going 1-0 as Washington won its first championship.

Here are the totals Scherzer has accumulated in the four playoff games in which he appeared, which includes a 3.38 ERA in 112 innings pitched:

With Detroit, Scherzer won four straight division titles and made an appearance in the 2012 World Series.

Year	Series	Opponent	W	L	W-L%	ERA	G	GS	IP	H	R	ER	HR	BB	SO	WHIP
2011	ALDS	NYY	1	0	1.000	1.27	2	1	7.1	4	1	1	0	4	7	1.127
2011	ALCS	TEX	0	1	0.000	10.00	2	2	8.1	11	9	9	1	5	7	1.975
2012	ALDS	OAK	0	0	0.000	0.00	1	1	5.1	3	1	0	0	1	8	0.784
2012	ALCS	NYY	1	0	1.000	1.73	1	1	5.2	2	1	1	0	2	10	0.769
2012	WS	SFG	0	0	0.000	4.43	1	1	6.1	7	3	3	1	1	8	1.311
2013	ALDS	OAK	2	0	1.000	3.00	2	1	9.0	6	3	3	1	4	13	1.111
2013	ALCS	BOS	0	1	0.000	2.75	2	2	13.1	6	4	4	0	7	21	0.992
2014	ALDS	BAL	0	1	0.000	6.34	1	1	7.1	7	5	5	2	1	6	1.127
2016	NLDS	LAD	0	1	0.000	3.75	2	2	12.0	10	5	5	3	2	12	1.000
2017	NLDS	CHC	0	1	0.000	3.80	2	1	7.1	4	5	3	0	4	8	1.127
2019	NLWC	MIL	0	0	NA	5.40	1	1	5.0	4	3	3	2	6	3	1.400
2019	NLDS	LAD	1	0	1.000	1.13	2	1	8.0	4	1	1	0	3	10	.875
2019	NLCS	STL	1	0	1.000	0.00	1	1	7.0	1	0	0	0	2	11	.429
2019	WS	HOU	1	0	1.000	3.60	2	2	10	12	4	4	1	7	10	1.900
TOTALS			7	5	0.583	3.38	22	18	112.0	81	45	42	12	46	137	1.134

STACKED STAFFS

Scherzer has a career that stands out among the best pitchers in the league. He **toiled** seven years pitching in the NL (Arizona, two years; Washington, five seasons) and five seasons in the AL pitching for the Detroit Tigers. His numbers through 2019 are almost equally split between the two leagues:

League	W	L	W-L%	ERA	G	GS	IP	H	R	ER	HR	BB	SO	WHIP
AL	82	35	0.701	3.52	161	161	1011.6	908	420	396	108	305	1081	1.199
NL	88	54	0.620	2.94	204	195	1277.0	975	456	417	146	313	1611	1.009
TOTALS	170	89	0.656	3.20	365	356	2290.0	1883	876	813	254	618	2692	1.092

Scherzer has had the opportunity to pitch on the same staff as some of the best pitchers in MLB. He began his career with the Arizona Diamondbacks, where in 2008 he pitched alongside Hall of Fame pitcher Randy Johnson, whose 4,875 strikeouts are the most by a left-handed pitcher in league history and second most behind Nolan Ryan's 5,714. Other great pitchers that he has shared a bullpen with in his career include:

- Justin Verlander (2010–2014, Detroit)
- David Price (2014, Detroit)
- Stephen Strasburg (2015–2019, Washington)

Among all of these pitchers, there is one Hall of Fame enshrinement (Johnson, 2015), 33 All-Star appearances (Johnson, 10; Verlander, 8; Scherzer, 7; Price, 5; Strasburg, 3), 19 season strikeout leaders (Johnson, 9; Verlander, 5; Scherzer, 3; Price and Strasburg, 1 each), 11 Cy Young Awards (Johnson, 5; Scherzer, 3; Verlander, 2; Price, 1), three World Series championships (Johnson, Price, Scherzer, Strasburg and Verlander, 1 each), and six no-hitters pitched (Johnson, Scherzer, and Verlander, 2 each).

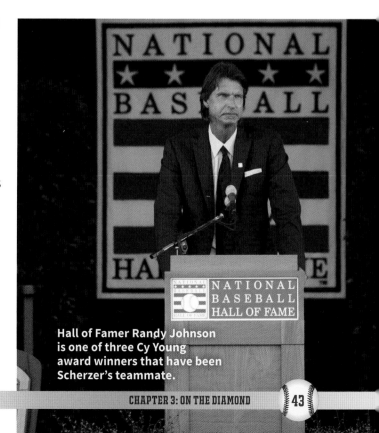

Hall of Famer Randy Johnson is one of three Cy Young award winners that have been Scherzer's teammate.

Here is how the careers of these great arms (and current and former teammates of Scherzer) compare to each other:

	W	L	W-L%	ERA	G	GS	IP	H	R	ER	HR	BB	SO	WHIP
Johnson	303	166	0.646	3.29	618	603	4135.1	3346	1703	1513	411	1497	4875	1.171
Verlander	225	129	0.636	3.33	453	453	2982.0	2535	1190	1103	308	850	3006	1.135
Scherzer	170	89	0.656	3.20	365	356	2290.0	1883	876	813	254	618	2692	1,092
Price	150	80	0.652	3.31	321	311	2029.2	1813	819	746	207	527	1981	1.153
Strasburg	112	58	0.659	3.17	239	239	1438.2	1185	557	506	143	377	1695	1.086

Justin Verlander played with Scherzer in Detroit. In 2011, he won the Triple Crown, Cy Young and MVP.

TEXT-DEPENDENT QUESTIONS

1. How many times did Scherzer win the Cy Young Award?
   When did he win his first Cy Young Award?

2. How many times did he lead his league in strikeouts?

3. What is Scherzer's career ERA?

 RESEARCH PROJECT

One of the best statistics kept for a pitcher is his walks and hits per nine-innings pitched average. The WHIP is a good measurement of how many times a pitcher keeps runners off base per innings pitched. Scherzer boasts a career WHIP of 1.100, which is low for a pitcher. It isn't, however, the lowest for pitchers in the history of the league. Do some research to determine the lowest single-season and career WHIP. Determine also where Scherzer ranks on the career list for WHIP average and where his lowest single-season WHIP ranks.

WORDS TO UNDERSTAND

acquisition: the act of coming into possession, ownership, or control of something

context: the parts of a written or spoken statement that precede or follow a specific word or passage, usually influencing its meaning or effec

set-up men: the common term for the pitchers who might pitch in a gam between the starter and the closer

speculation: conjectural consideration of a matter; conjecture

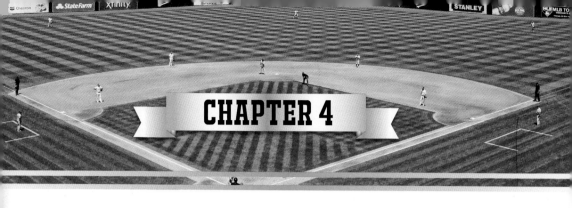

WORDS COUNT

When the time comes to address the media before or after a game, players either retreat to the comfort of traditional phrases that avoid controversy (Cliché City), or they speak their minds with refreshing candor (Quote Machine).

Here are 10 quotes, compiled in part from websites with some insight as to the **context** of what Scherzer is talking about or referencing:

"**We've had three years of success. We've never really been recognized this early. We've always been picked (low to start), and then we always went out and surprised everybody. Well, now somebody has said we should do well this year. . . . Obviously we have the opportunity to take it up a level, but it is on this year.**"

The Washington Nationals have experienced success as a team beginning in the 2012 season. This was after drafting Cy Young-winning pitcher Stephen Strasburg in 2009 with the number one overall pick and NL MVP Bryce Harper (Philadelphia Phillies) in 2010. The **acquisition** of Scherzer in 2015, a three-time Cy Young winner, was the icing on top of the cake that has helped keep the team at or near the top of the NL East Division through 2018. The team averaged 93 wins and 69 losses in the three seasons prior to Scherzer joining the team, finishing in first in 2012 and 2014. His joining the team in 2015 fueled **speculation** that the Nationals would go further than the NL Division Series, (NLDS) which failed to happen in 2014. Although they did not make the playoffs, his quote suggests that expectations should be kept in the context of the current season.

Rating: Quote Machine

Nationals Park became home for Scherzer when he signed with Washington in 2014.

> ## "It's a funny game. Sometimes it's the little things that don't go your way. As a pitching staff, we are just going out there and try to throw up zeros because we know we want the next guy to go up and put up zeros. Everybody is trying to pull up each other."

Success in the game comes first from the pitching mound. Scherzer recognizes that his job as a starter is to get outs and limit the number of runs the other team scores. Putting up "zeros" makes it easier for the next pitchers, the **set-up men** and closers, to finish the game and secure victory. Scherzer, in this quote, talks about the things he has to do as a starting pitcher to make the job easier for the next "guy" who comes up after him to win the game. **Rating: Quote Machine**

> ## "Social media is dangerous for baseball players. Things can get taken out of context so fast. You can say something you don't want to say. It's dangerous."

Scherzer, as an older player (age 34 as of start of 2019 season), is not a big user of social media. He maintains a Twitter account (@Max_Scherzer) and an Instagram account (@maxscherzer31), but for the most part, he stays away from posting many of his thoughts and opinions online. He knows that things written on social media can often be taken out of context. He had so many problems with his Twitter account being hacked that in late October 2018, he posted his intention to leave Twitter and Instagram. He did not delete the accounts, but between October of 2018 and the end of the 2019 season, Scherzer has only tweeted once, sending out a post thanking the Nationals Foundation for supporting the cause of animal rescue. **Rating: Quote Machine**

"That's the thing—7–0 is a nice thing, but I don't really hang my hat on that. If I was 0–7 and still pitching well, giving my team a chance to win, I'd still be proud of it. For me, it's all about going out there and making sure I'm going deep into games, keeping their offense down. I've been doing that for the most part this year."

Scherzer's 2013 season with the Tigers began with a perfect seven wins and no losses. It was a phenomenal beginning for Scherzer that would end with 21 wins and the AL Cy Young Award. His effort that season, which included 240

Scherzer started the 2013 season 7–0 with Detroit. He went on to finish the season 21–3 and won the Cy Young award.

strikeouts, a win–loss percentage of 0.875 and a WHIP of 0.972 (both tops in the AL), helped lead the Tigers into the AL Championship Series (ALCS) against the Boston Red Sox. His pat response about going deep in games notwithstanding, Scherzer did continue his dominance for the entire season. **Rating: Cliché City**

"Strikeouts are sexy. To punch out 20 batters is sexy."

Scherzer faced his former Detroit Tiger team as a member of the Washington Nationals in a May 11, 2016, game. The game was an incredible display of his power and control as a pitcher as he mowed down 20 Tigers batters on his way to tying the major league record for most strikeouts in a

Roger Clemens is one of only two pitchers in MLB history other than Scherzer to strike out 20 batters in a nine-inning game.

nine-inning game. Scherzer became the first pitcher to accomplish this in 18 years, tying former Chicago Cubs pitcher Kerry Woods, who struck out 20 on May 6, 1998, and Roger Clemens of the Boston Red Sox, who struck out 20 batters twice in his career. Scherzer made this comment when asked about the feeling that comes with striking out 20 batters. **Rating: Quote Machine**

> **"For everyone coming back, for all the things we have going for this program— the talent, the makeup—you've got to feel that we have a shot to get to Omaha. It'd be taking this program up that big step, that next level. We want to do that. For Hunter and Culp, it's the same thing. You're not playing for the draft. You're playing for Omaha."**

This quote comes from Scherzer's days as a member of the University of Missouri Tigers baseball team. During his three years at Missouri, he appeared in the NCAA College World Series playoffs each year (2004–2006). The quote refers to his desire to go deep in the playoffs and make it all the way to the championship game, which in past years was held at Creighton University in Omaha, Nebraska. He felt that the Tigers team that came back together in 2006, featuring fellow All Big 12 player Nathan Culp and outfielder Hunter Mense. The team advanced to the Super Regional, where their college careers ended against Cal-State Fullerton. **Rating: Quote Machine**

> ### "Normally when I look at stuff, I try to look at the good things. When I watch video, I try to watch the good starts so I can see how my mechanics are in those."

Scherzer is a student of the game and likes to study his pitching. When looking at a past pitching performance, he likes to focus on the good parts of his throwing motion, the way he strikes batters out, and how consistent he is in throwing pitches from inning to inning. His focus on mechanics, the way he delivers a pitch across the plate, is an important part of his preparation for future starts. It helps him memorize the good and put in his mind those motions that have helped him become one of the most dominant pitchers on the mound. **Rating: Quote Machine**

Scherzer constantly watches video of his games to study his mechanics.

"If you look at it from the macro side, who'd people rather see hit—Big Papi or me? Who would people rather see, a real hitter hitting home runs or a pitcher swinging a wet newspaper? Both leagues need to be on the same set of rules."

Scherzer made this comment talking about his desire to see the designated hitter used in the NL, as it has been used in the AL since 1973. He made this comment as he was leaving the AL's Detroit Tigers at the end of the

When he was a pitcher with Detroit in the American League, Scherzer preferred that the fans did not have to watch him hit.

2014 season after signing a seven-year, $210 million contract with the NL's Washington Nationals. This also touched off a war of words between Scherzer and San Francisco Giants ace Madison Bumgarner, one of the better-hitting pitchers in MLB. Bumgarner, who in 2014 was the first pitcher since 1966 to hit a grand slam home run, felt that Scherzer's comment disrespected pitchers who can hit and pointed out that Scherzer knew that hitting was a requirement when he signed his contract with the Nationals. **Rating: Quote Machine**

"**What bugs me is the whole process is about tearing you down. You have to have some resolve in yourself to continue to believe what you bring to the team, the field, and the clubhouse. I understand the process is hard, and it's only gotten harder.**"

This quote from Scherzer refers to the contract process and how it can be hard on players trying to stay loyal to their teams and the fans, but also get paid what they believe they are worth. There are few three-time Cy Young Award winners in the league, especially one averaging nearly 276 strikeouts a season and on his way to joining the 3,000-strikeout club (with plenty of years left to play). Scherzer expressed some frustration with the process of signing his seven-year deal with the Nationals, the back-and-forth between

GOING DEEP

He may not like to hit, but he has a home run.

Scherzer signed a seven-year, $210 million deal with the Washington Nationals in 2015, which moved him from the AL to the NL. It meant that he would have to hit for the first time since leaving Arizona in 2007. Scherzer, known as player who favors the NL adopting the same designated hitter (DH) rule that the AL has, showed that he was ready to accept this part of his role as an NL player in an August 1, 2017, game against the Miami Marlins. Scherzer took Marlins pitcher Chris O'Grady deep for a three-run home run in the top of the second inning. The hit was his first career home run, and it put aside any question of his willingness to swing a bat.

After 262 career at bats (with the Arizona Diamondbacks and Washington Nationals), Scherzer crushes a pitch 381 feet (116.13 m) for his first career major league home run.

team management and his agent, and how much harder signing a contract has become compared to when he first received an offer in 2006 from the Arizona Diamondbacks. **Rating: Quote Machine**

Scherzer has been a star with Washington, but he says the process of getting a contract signed there was difficult.

"We talked about this, and it happened in Cincinnati, so I don't know if we were playing them, but he'll grunt when he [Nats Reliever Shawn Kelley] throws a fastball. But I don't like it when he grunts and he only throws it 92. I say if he grunts, he at least has to throw it 95."

Scherzer remarked on how former teammate Shawn Kelley (Texas Rangers) grunts when throwing a fastball. Maybe the grunting helps him with his process of throwing a 95-mile-per-hour (153 kilometers-per-hour) pitch. Scherzer jokingly indicates that when he grunts, he doesn't particularly care for the sound, but if that's what it takes for Kelley to throw a hard fastball, he's fine with the grunting.

Scherzer is not fond of former Nationals teammate Shawn Kelley's tendency to grunt when he pitches.

TEXT-DEPENDENT QUESTIONS

1. When did Scherzer hit his first career home run? Who was the team he was playing against?

2. What was the value of the contract Scherzer signed in 2015 to join the Washington Nationals? How many years is the contract?

3. At what speed did Scherzer prefer former teammate Shawn Kelley to throw the ball before he would be OK with his grunting?

RESEARCH PROJECT

Pitchers who can hit are a dual threat in baseball. There have been many pitchers throughout the years who have shown their ability to be effective in the batter's box swinging the bat as well as when they are throwing strikes. Look at all of the pitchers who have swung the bat since the 1985 MLB season. List all of the pitchers with at least a 0.200 batting average, and determine which ones hit the most home runs, stole the most bases, had the highest batting average, and received a Silver Slugger award for their efforts as a hitter.

WORDS TO UNDERSTAND

formidable: causing fear, apprehension, or dread

influential: having or exerting the capacity or power of persons or things to be a compelling force or produce effects on the actions, behavior, opinions, etc., of others

sabermetrics: the application of statistical analysis to baseball records, especially to evaluate and compare the performance of individual players

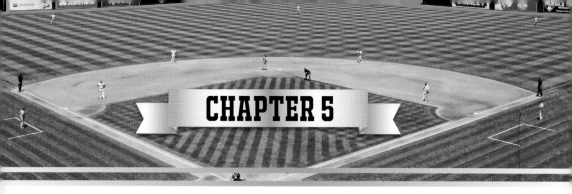

CHAPTER 5

OFF THE DIAMOND

MAX SCHERZER'S EDUCATION

Scherzer went to school at the University of Missouri at Columbia. He started his studies at Missouri as a freshman in 2004, majoring in business finance. He was inspired to go into that major by his brother Alex, who studied business and economics at Missouri. It also helped that Scherzer scored a 35 out of 36 points on the math section of his ACT examination and has a genuine interest and love for math. In fact, he is one of the few pitchers in MLB who uses what is known as **sabermetrics** to study his performance and analyze the results of his pitching.

While attending the University of Missouri and playing on the baseball team, he met his future wife Erica May. Erica May Scherzer was a pitcher on the Missouri women's softball team, making them a **formidable** couple on the mound. A heart condition forced Erica May to stop competing at the collegiate level. Scherzer, who left school after his junior year in 2006 when the Arizona Diamondbacks drafted him, did not finish his degree. His wife, who also attended the University of Colorado in Boulder prior to coming to Columbia, did graduate with a degree in history. The couple married in 2013.

SCHERZER'S HOME AND FAMILY

Scherzer and Erica May make their home in the wealthy and **influential** Washington, D.C., suburb of McLean, Virginia. McLean, which is 8 miles (13 km) northwest of D.C., is the home of many politicians, foreign and domestic diplomats, and sports stars, including Washington Capitals (National Hockey League) captain Alex Ovechkin, and Washington Wizards (National Basketball Association) star Bradley Beal. It is also home to Hickory Hill, the famous home of former President John F. and Jackie Kennedy and later former Attorney

Scherzer (2nd from right) attends an event to celebrate the success of the Save Vanishing Species postal stamp. The stamp, featuring an Amur tiger design, raised more than two million dollars for the Wildlife Without Borders Multinational Species Conservation Funds.

General and Senator Robert and Ethel Kennedy. The home was the scene of several famous photographs from the late 1950s of the families playing touch football with their children. The Scherzers welcomed a daughter, Brooklyn May, in November of 2017.

Scherzer's parents Brad and Jan raised him in Chesterfield, Missouri, a suburb of St. Louis, along with his younger brother Alex. Alex, who also attended the University of Missouri, was every bit a math freak as his older sibling. Unfortunately, the younger Scherzer succumbed to a battle with depression and committed suicide on June 21, 2013. Scherzer has dedicated every start since that date to the memory of his younger brother.

HOW SCHERZER GIVES BACK TO THE COMMUNITY

The Scherzers are financially comfortable with his signing of a multiyear contract worth $210 million with the Nationals. The financial security that he has received as a result of the deal gives Scherzer the flexibility to speak on the behalf of several organizations that he cares about. He has been actively involved in the communities he has pitched in, including Detroit and Washington, D.C.

Some of the charities and efforts that Scherzer supports include the following:

- *Humane Society of the United States* is one of the oldest animal rights advocacy organizations in the country. Founded in 1959, the mission of the group is to stop animal cruelty and provide a better life for our animal friends. This includes direct care and assistance to animals in need, working with local societies for the prevention of cruelty to animals, and helping pass and enforce laws against the cruelty of animals. The Scherzers, who are pet owners and vocal in their support for animal rights, participate in advocacy efforts from their Washington, D.C., home (and its closeness to the U.S. Capitol and seat of power) and produce videos that make public appeals for funding and support.

- *Human Rescue Alliance* is a 501c3 organization similar to the Humane Society regarding animal protection goals. The Human Rescue Alliance focuses on the needs of homeless cats and dogs, particularly those displaced by natural disasters. The Scherzers' efforts on behalf of the Human Rescue Alliance include the sale of the Max Scherzer Human Rescue Alliance baseball shirt, the proceeds from which support the efforts of the organization.

- *Polaris Project* an organization founded in 2002, it takes its name from that given to the North Star, a guide used by southern slaves to guide them northward to freedom. The project works to end human slavery and trafficking (the illegal sale of humans to others), a global problem that affects the lives of more than 40,000 victims a year. The Scherzers have been involved in hosting fund-raising campaigns, the Autographs & Athletes program of MLB, and the Strike Out Modern Slavery effort, which raised nearly $65,000 for the organization based on the number of strikeouts Scherzer threw in the 2016 season.

In addition to these charities, Scherzer, through the Washington Nationals Dream Foundation, has supported other community-based efforts on behalf of disadvantaged youth in the Washington, D.C., area.

- *Washington Nationals Dream Foundation* is the charitable organization of the team involved in providing funding and support for Washington, D.C., area-based initiatives and programs that benefit children and youth. Scherzer organizes a fantasy baseball league where proceeds go to specifically support the efforts of the Dream Foundation:

  - *Nationals Youth Baseball Academy*, located in the Southeast section of D.C., provides an opportunity for disadvantaged youth to gain access to professional-level sports fields and classrooms to develop their skills, participate in general fitness programs, and receive academic support.

Miss District of Columbia Kate Grinold makes an appearance at the 2008 Washington Nationals Dream Foundation gala. The Foundation supports community-based efforts to help local disadvantaged youth.

  - *Big League Impact Global Fund* represents an effort of MLB to raise money for global communities in need. It has raised $3.1 million, supported 45 charities, funded 63 individual projects, and affected the lives of more than 640,000 people around the world.

A FRIEND TO ALL ANIMALS

Scherzer's family includes several rescue animals that the Scherzers have acquired through their mutual love for pets. The four dogs and two cats that live with the family are an important part of their life's work to help people and animals live together and reduce the number of pets that end up in animal shelters. They support several organizations that are dedicated to the health and well being of animals, including the Humane Society of America and Human Rescue Alliance. Scherzer is so committed to animal welfare that he agreed to pay the adoption fees for D.C.-area residents who were looking to adopt animals displaced by 2017's Hurricane Harvey. More than 100 pets were placed in new homes as a result of his generosity.

Scherzer demonstrates his unquestionable support for animals and their lives through his support of the Humane Society of the United States in this 2016 public service announcement.

THE REPRESENTATION OF SCHERZER

Sports super agent Scott Boras of the Boras Corporation represents Scherzer. A former MLB prospect in the 1970s (who attended the University of Pacific and holds several offensive records for the school), Boras is considered one of the best agents in the game when it comes to getting every dollar for his client. It was Boras' effort working with Washington Nationals front office personnel that landed Scherzer his seven-year deal with the team. Not only does Boras represent Scherzer, but he is also the agent of former Nationals star Bryce Harper, who signed a 13-year, $330 million deal with the Philadelphia Phillies prior to the start of the 2019 season.

Scherzer's agent is Scott Boras, one of the most powerful agents in pro sports.

SALARY INFORMATION

Scherzer and Boras came to terms on a new contract with the Nationals in 2015. The multiyear (seven) deal is worth $210 million, which made him at the time the highest paid right-handed pitcher in major league history. The contract included a combination of base salary, bonuses, and performance incentives for things like winning the Cy Young Award, MVP, and All-Star game appearances.

The contract that Scherzer and his agent Boras orchestrated is back-loaded, which means that a portion of the salary owed him by the Nationals is scheduled to be paid after the contract period is over. He accepted a deferral in salary for half ($105 million) of the $210 million, which will be paid between 2022 and 2028. It will give Scherzer and his family (and any of the animals he plans to rescue long after his pitching career is over) financial security for years to come.

Here is a breakdown of Scherzer's salary earnings since receiving a signing bonus of $3 million from the Arizona Diamondbacks in 2006:

Season	Team (League)	Salary	Bonus	Total Amount
2006	Arizona Diamondbacks (NL)	$0	$3,000,000	$3,000,000
2007	Arizona Diamondbacks (NL)	$950,000	$0	$950,000
2008	Arizona Diamondbacks (NL)	$950,000	$0	$950,000
2009	Detroit Tigers (AL)	$1,450,000	$0	$1,450,000
2010	Detroit Tigers (AL)	$950,000	$0	$950,000
2011	Detroit Tigers (AL)	$600,000	$0	$600,000

Year	Team	Salary	Bonuses/Deferred	Total
2012	Detroit Tigers (AL)	$3,750,000	$0	$3,750,000
2013	Detroit Tigers (AL)	$6,725,000	$0	$6,725,000
2014	Detroit Tigers (AL)	$15,525,000	$0	$15,525,000
2015*	Washington Nationals (NL)	$10,000,000	$5,175,000	$15,175,000
2016	Washington Nationals (NL)	$15,000,000	$100,000	$15,100,000
2017	Washington Nationals (NL)	$15,000,000	$0	$15,000,000
2018	Washington Nationals (NL)	$15,000,000	$100,000	$15,100,000
2019	Washington Nationals (NL)	$0	$15,000,000	$15,000,000
2020	Washington Nationals (NL)	$0	$15,000,000	$15,000,000
2021	Washington Nationals (NL)	$0	$15,000,000	$15,000,000
2022+	Washington Nationals (NL)	$15,000,000	$0	$15,000,000
2023+	Washington Nationals (NL)	$15,000,000	$0	$15,000,000
2024+	Washington Nationals (NL)	$15,000,000	$0	$15,000,000
2025+	Washington Nationals (NL)	$15,000,000	$0	$15,000,000
2026+	Washington Nationals (NL)	$15,000,000	$0	$15,000,000
2027+	Washington Nationals (NL)	$15,000,000	$0	$15,000,000
2028+	Washington Nationals (NL)	$15,000,000	$0	$15,000,000
TOTALS		$190,900,000	$53,375,000	$244,275,000

*Scherzer signed a seven-year contract with the Nationals in 2015 worth $210.0 million, which included a signing bonus of $50 million.

+The contract included $105.5 million in deferred salary (and bonuses) to be paid over the years 2022–2028. He becomes an unrestricted free agent at the end of the 2021 MLB season. Incentive bonuses were available for All-Star game appearances, Cy Young Awards, and league and World Series MVP honors.

The Nationals need the crowds to keep coming at Nationals Park to pay Scherzer all of the $210 million they owe him through 2028.

Scherzer has made World Series appearances as both a member of the Detroit Tigers and the Washington Nationals. He is serious about looking at the numbers, studying his mechanics, and doing everything he can to be competitive and keep his team in the game. Scherzer has had the type of career that many players can only dream of. Even after 12 seasons in the league, there does not appear to be any letting up for Mad Max. Looking at his numbers, he will finish his career as one of the most dominant pitchers in the history of the game.

Scherzer is on pace to be a sure-fire hall of famer by the time he retires.

MAX SCHERZER

TEXT-DEPENDENT QUESTIONS

1. How much of his 2015 contract salary with the Washington Nationals was deferred? For how many years?

2. What animal rescue organizations does Scherzer support?

3. How did Scherzer and his wife Erica May meet? What is the name of the Scherzer's daughter? When was she born?

 # RESEARCH PROJECT

The Scherzers, Max and Erica May, met while both playing college athletics at the University of Missouri. Looking at the league over the past 25 seasons, research and find 10 examples of players whose wives also played varsity sports at the same school (i.e., women's volleyball, softball, soccer, basketball, etc.).

SERIES GLOSSARY
OF KEY TERMS

All-Star: a player chosen by fans and managers to play on the All-Star team against the opposing league in the MLB All-Star game in the middle of the season. The league that wins hosts the first game of the World Series.

box: the rectangle where the batter stands or the area where the pitcher fields the ball; also called the batter's box.

breaking ball: any pitch that curves in the air: a curve ball, slider, screwball, sinker, or forkball.

bunt: a ball batted for a short distance to help the batter to reach first base or to advance another runner on base while the defense makes the out at first.

change-up: a slow pitch that throws off a batter's timing.

cleanup: the fourth hitter in the lineup, usually the best hitter on the team. If all three runners get on base before the cleanup hitter, it's up to him to get them home, likely with a home run.

closer: the pitcher called in during the last innings to preserve a lead.

curve: a pitch that spins the ball with a snap of the wrist, forcing it to curve near the plate.

Cy Young Award: the award given annually to the pitcher in each of the American and National Leagues deemed to be the most outstanding in the regular season. The award winner is determined by votes cast by the Baseball Writers' Association of America, a professional association for baseball journalists.

designated hitter (DH): the player who hits for the pitcher. This position was created in 1973 and is used only in the American League.

double play: two outs in one play, for example, a strikeout and a base runner being thrown out or when two runners are called out on the bases.

doubleheader: when two teams play twice on the same day, one game after the other.

earned run average (ERA): ERA is a pitching statistic that measures the average number of earned runs scored against a pitcher for every nine innings pitched.

error: a defensive mistake resulting in a batter reaching base or getting extra bases. The official scorer calls errors.

fastball: a pitch thrown at high speed, usually more than 90 miles per hour (145 km/h) in MLB.

foul ball: when the ball is hit into foul territory. A hitter's first two fouls count as strikes, but a batter can't be called out on a foul ball.

Gold Glove Award: the Gold Glove is given annually to the player at each position in both the American and National Leagues deemed to have exhibited superior fielding performance in the regular season. Votes cast by the team managers and coaches determine the award winner.

grand slam: a home run when runners are on all the bases.

ground-rule double: when a ball is hit fairly but then goes out of play (e.g., over the home run fence after it bounces) but because of an agreed-upon rule for the ball park, the player gets to second base.

hit-and-run: a play in which a base runner runs right when the pitcher pitches, and the hitter tries to hit the ball into play to help the runner get two bases or avoid a double play.

knuckleball: a pitch with as little spin as possible that moves slowly and unpredictably. The pitcher grips the ball with his fingertips or knuckles when throwing the pitch.

line drive: when a batter hits the ball hard and low into the field of play, sometimes called "a rope."

Most Valuable Player (MVP) Award: the MVP award is given annually to the player in each of the American and National Leagues deemed to be the most valuable to his team in the regular season. The award winner is determined by votes cast by the Baseball Writers' Association of America, a professional association for baseball journalists.

no-hitter: a game in which one team gets no base hits.

pickoff: when a pitcher or catcher throws a runner out, catching him or her standing off the base.

relief pitcher: a pitcher who comes into the game to replace another pitcher.

sacrifice: when a batter makes an out on purpose to advance a runner (e.g., a sacrifice bunt or fly ball). A sacrifice play is not an official at bat for the hitter.

Silver Slugger Award: given annually to the player at each position in each of the American and National Leagues deemed to be the best offensive player in the regular season. Votes cast by the team managers and coaches determine the award winner.

slider: a pitch that is almost as fast as a fastball but curves. The pitcher tries to confuse the batter, who may have trouble deciding what kind of pitch is coming.

stolen base: when a base runner runs right when the pitcher pitches, and if the pitch is not hit, makes it to the next base before being thrown out.

strike zone: the area above home plate where strikes are called. The pitch must be over home plate, above the batter's knees, and below the batter's belt.

strikeout: when a batter gets a third strike, either by missing the ball or not swinging on a pitch that is in the strike zone.

trade deadline: the trade deadline, which typically falls at 4 p.m. ET on July 31, is the last point during the regular season at which players can be traded from one club to another.

walk: when the pitcher throws four pitches outside the strike zone (called balls by the umpire) before throwing three strikes, allowing the hitter to walk to first base.

WAR: this acronym stands for Wins Above Replacement. It is an advanced statistics metric designed to measure the value of a player by indicating how many games a player adds to a team's win total versus those that would be added by the best available replacement player. For position players, the formula is WAR = (Batting Runs + Base Running Runs + Fielding Runs + Positional Adjustment + League Adjustment + Replacement Runs) / (Runs per Win). For pitchers, the formula is WAR = [[(((League "FIP" − "FIP") / Pitcher Specific Runs per Win] + Replacement Level) (IP/9)] Leverage Multiplier for Relievers] + League Correction.

wild pitch: A pitcher is charged with a wild pitch when his pitch is so errant that the catcher is unable to control it, and as a result, the base runner(s) advance.

FURTHER READING

Baseball Prospectus. *2019 Nationals Prospectus: A Baseball Companion: Washington Nationals.* Sterling, Virginia: Stylus Publishing, LLC, 2019.

Carroll, Ian. *Everything You Ever Wanted to Know about Washington Nationals.* Scotts Valley, California: CreateSpace Independent Publishing Platform, 2017.

Dorfman, H. A. *The Mental ABCs of Pitching: A Handbook for Performance Enhancement.* Lanham, Maryland: Globe Pequot, 2017.

Gage, Tom. *The Big 50: Detroit Tigers: The Men and Moments That Made the Detroit Tigers.* Chicago, Illinois: Triumph Books, 2017.

Pappu, Sridhar. *The Year of the Pitcher: Bob Gibson, Denny McClain, and the End of Baseball's Golden Age.* Boston, Massachusetts: Houghton Mifflin Harcourt, 2017.

INTERNET RESOURCES

https://www.baseball-reference.com/players/s/scherma01.shtml
The baseball-specific resource provided by Sports Reference LLC for current and historical statistics of Max Scherzer.

https://bleacherreport.com/mlb
The official website for Bleacher Report Sport's MLB reports on each of the 30 teams.

https://www.cbssports.com/mlb/teams/WAS/washington-nationals/
The web page for the Washington Nationals, provided by CBSSports.com, providing the latest news and information, player profiles, scheduling, and standings.

https://www.washingtonpost.com/sports/nationals/?utm_term=.08ef96b05028
The web page of the *Washington Post* newspaper for the Washington Nationals baseball team.

http://www.espn.com/mlb/team/_/name/wsh/washington-nationals
The official website of ESPN sports network for the Washington Nationals.

https://www.mlb.com/
The official website of MLB.

https://www.mlb.com/nationals
The official MLB website for the Washington Nationals baseball team, including history, player information, statistics, and news.

https://sports.yahoo.com/mlb/
The official website of Yahoo! Sports MLB coverage, providing news, statistics, and important information about the association and its 30 teams.

INDEX

INDEX

INDEX

AUTHOR BIOGRAPHY

Donald Parker is an avid sports fan, author, and father. He enjoys watching and participating in many types of sports, including football, basketball, baseball, and golf. He enjoyed a brief career as a punter and defensive back at NCAA Division III Carroll College (now University) in Waukesha, Wisconsin, and spends much of his time now watching and writing about the sports he loves.

PHOTO CREDITS

PHOTO CREDITS

EDUCATIONAL VIDEO LINKS

Chapter 1:

http://x-qr.net/1JJ4

http://x-qr.net/1Lnm

http://x-qr.net/1Kb0

http://x-qr.net/1K8s

http://x-qr.net/1KGm

http://x-qr.net/1J7c

http://x-qr.net/1Ks3

http://x-qr.net/1Jyt

Chapter 2:

http://x-qr.net/1KBE

Chapter 3:

http://x-qr.net/1LZV

Chapter 4:

http://x-qr.net/1JBi

Chapter 5:

http://x-qr.net/1KEj